T0345910

Fix Quiet

Also by John Poch:

Dolls

Two Men Fighting with a Knife

Ghost Towns of the Enchanted Circle

Hockey Haiku: The Essential Collection

Poems

In Defense of the Fall

Fix Quiet

POEMS

John Poch

WINNER OF THE NEW CRITERION POETRY PRIZE

St. Augustine's Press
SOUTH BEND, IN 2015

Funding for this year's New Criterion Poetry Prize
has been provided by Joy & Michael Millette

www.staugustine.net
Library of Congress Cataloging-in-Publication Data:

Poch, John Evans, 1966–
    [Poems. Selections]
    Fix Quiet : Poems / John Poch. — 1st Edition.
        pages cm
    "Winner of the New Criterion Poetry Prize."
    ISBN 978-1-58731-269-4 (clothbound: alk. paper)
    I. Title.
PS3616.O28A6 2015
811'.6 – dc23   2015005865

Contents

For James, Cherie, and Judith, believers

Acknowledgments

Alabama Literary Review: "Four Riddles"
America: "Ignored Woodwork in Old Churches"
American Literary Review: "Drama Major"
Birmingham Poetry Review: "At Dante's Tomb"
Carbon Copy Magazine: "Brief Aubade"
Carolina Quarterly: "The Little Rio Grande," "Pot Creek" &
　　　"River Prayer"
Cellpoems: "Potential"
Chronicle of Higher Education blog: "Echo"
The City: "Good God" & "Memento Mori"
The Formalist: "Et Cetera"
Gray's Sporting Journal: " 'Trout that Swim' "
Image: "Ars Proverbium" & "The Race of the Candles"
Linebreak: "Liquid Italy"
Poetry: "Elegy for a Suicide"
Sewanee Theological Review: "For the Christian Angler"
Smartish Pace: "At the Hospice"
Southwest Review: "The Rio Hondo"
storySouth: "A Crown for Meghan"
Thrush Poetry Journal: "Cause," *"Duck and Cover,"* "The Rio
　　　Grande" & "Sonnet on Time"
Unsplendid: "Invisible Fish," "Nathaniel Hawthorne at Niagara
　　　Falls" & "Pope Innocent X"
Yale Review: "Perspective on Might"

"Fall" appeared in *Fashioned Pleasures: Twenty-Four Poets Play Bouts-
　　　Rimés with a Shakespearean Sonnet*

This book was made possible by a generous CAHSS grant and
development leave from Texas Tech University, a grant from the
Fulbright U.S. Scholar Program, and a residency from Fundación
Valparaiso in Mojácar, Spain.

Fix Quiet

But one of the soldiers with a spear pierced His side,
and forthwith came there out blood and water.
  —John 19:34

Because I could not say it—
I fixed it in the Verse—
  —Emily Dickinson

Shrike

Poetry clutches the dead branch
a predatory bird prefers.
Or prey on the lookout.
This is a story of listening
as dry thorns in a thicket might
wait beyond their own death
for another flesh.
And this is a song that fixes
quiet, a song of earth below
and wind across the cactus spine
compelling the locust to shine.
Who pins the barbed beetle
on barbed wire like an icon
honoring Saint Hunger?

Poetry is found singly,
less buoyant than imagined.

I

Kick Me

And my poor fool is hang'd! No, no, no life!
—King Lear

Dumb clod of an earth-bound clown
not long for this three-ring town,
in the stands, I act a little blind.
The crowd bombards me from behind
with popcorn, empty cups,
and kicks (I pretend to eat it up,
for kicks). Sometimes a tug at my cuffs,
one little hand innocuous
as a starfish washing up on waves.
But this curious awe withdraws,
crawls back to the warm caves
made of laps and arms. Because
I earn my keep from failure,
I doubt at my mirror in the trailer.
I'm not supposed to talk. Ghostly,
going on a year, I've grown mostly
monkish, old, a cranky telephone
talking to myself, to Jesus.
And the big-shoe chump I am confuses
the agile would-be high trapezist.
Under the spotlight, I'm a lazy-Susaned
block of red cheddar with a knife
of brutally cute potential in it
marionetted for a minute.
They love to see me hang, survive,
and wonder how I darken, knocked cold

like a lighthouse, how I hold
my frown, how I try and try to try.
I'll climb the ladder like a swimmer.
I've got the morning glory tremor.
I know how high May days may be,
will come welcome and humming
and drop to waiting bridesmaids
a comedy of bright bouquets
like fireworks a long time coming.
But first, a mirror and a white face.
Who doesn't dig the ace of spades?
The simplest of comedians,
love is sacrificial, cool
as Cordelia's disobedience.
Something will come of nothing's fool.

Bacon

I'm in the kitchen waking by degrees,
cooking Saturday breakfast when I know,
against death's entropy, I serve a purpose
although I live in Lubbock, more or less
surviving, like a hockey penalty kill.
On NPR, if it isn't Kevin Bacon

on TV! What? I nearly burn the bacon.
On the stovetop, it's 350 degrees
or so. The coffee's kicking in. I'd kill
to nail that righteous state between the know-
ing and the waking Yeats suggested lest
one fall toward rhetoric, or merely purpose.

But me, I need the stress of math, of purpose,
the blessed rage for order that comes like bacon
from slaughter to table, stacked, fanned, packaged, less—
$5.99 a pound—than six degrees
farmer to truck to stockboy, clerk, me. No?
Yes. Listen, Romaine Gary of *Kill! Kill! Kill! Kill!*

links Christian Marquand whose dinner scene they kill
in *Apocalypse Now* (too much rhetorical purpose)
with Laurence Fishburne who starred with you-know-
who from *Mystic River*, bringing the Bacon
home. Silly. You don't need advanced degrees
to gather he's a lousy actor. Unless

you presume *Tremors* is the standard. Care less,
camp's more. Yet presumptive fallacies can kill
a claim. The slippery slope, for instance, degrees:
It's pig; it's not like slaughtering a porpoise!
A vegetarian . . . except for bacon,
I used to tell my friends at breakfast. *No*

meat for me, oh just eggs, but well, if no
one wants that last piece, I'll . . . Nevertheless,
witness this Texas license plate: MM BACN.
In Southern California, looks might kill
with a snooty rear-view glare of higher purpose
as they drive by in their hybrid, at thirty degrees—

their noses. On NPR, some rich pig kills
it at auction. Fat on content, artless on purpose:
Francis Bacon's oils. You can smell the grease.

Potential

The wine in the communion cup to the drunk.
The hospital handrail to the skater punk.

Four Riddles

after Greg Williamson

1.
I've come to call your body home.
We share the same blood and die alone.
I'll help you eat your ice cream cone.

2.
A hem is part of my resume.
I cloak with my hand what I have to say.
My hanky takes your breath away.

3.
Let's drink to homonyms: to two
as well as one. If you're looking to
see something more, then I am too.

4.
I tell the account that will be told.
It's safe to say I guard the gold
but cannot keep the change I hold.

1.
a. A parasite
b. Death
c. Your big brother
d. Your clogged artery

2.
a. a good seamstress
b. a cough
c. a magician
d. hanky-panky

3.
a. glasses
b. also
c. a weird personal ad
d. make it a double

4.
a. A teller
b. The till
c. A fortune teller
d. The pot at the end of the rainbow

Duck and Cover

The last of those to whom they showed the film,
we were amazed to see those children wait
like us, glued, floored, taut for the bomb's one fate
beneath the shelter of their desks. A kiln,
our classroom hardened us and set the glaze
of our eyes. Then recess came, and we harassed
the bone-thin boy with the yellow hair aghast
on his head like a worn-out plastic doll, mussed, crazed,
his scalp gone sissy pink with fright. Relentless
as rock and roll, we sang a mean refrain
and beat the drums of panic close to pain,
taunting the boy to duck and cover, friendless.

Fed up, he pulled his hair out, showed it to us,
shocked, the next generation's always clueless.

Drama Major

after "Ozymandias"

The less you stay at home, the less the land
will mean to you, they said. I packed a stone
for memory and luck. It turned to sand.
The more you smile, the less you'll later frown,
they smiled. It seemed half prayer and half command,
but I would not be swayed. In my face they read
the lines of grief, experience. What things
were not sheer artifice I was sure art fed.
So when my leading lady did appear,
she thought I was a god, a king of kings.
I told her stories fraught with wild despair,
of castles plagued by murders and decay.
I thought my gothic act could save her. Bare
your teeth, I said, like this. She ran away.

The Gideons Visit Local Junior High

The righteous question the immutable
for church and state, our holy separation.
No Darwin's ever read at a funeral,

or wedding feast or birth. The beautiful
old Bible chosen for inauguration—
the righteous question. The unmutable

old men stiff as Roman numerals,
red-lettered, over-underlined. Creation
knows Darwin's never read at a funeral.

The Word divides. Perhaps it's just inscrutable
literature at worst. But the damnation!
The righteous question the immutable:

one atheist angry as a fumarole,
they call her Old Faithful: *Imagine a nation
where Darwin's never read*! At a funeral

for God, men face the undisputable
fact that we suffer, die. With Job's privation,
the righteous question The Immutable.
No Darwin's ever read at a funeral.

Brief Aubade

The double standard still applies: for her
the walk of shame, for him the stride of pride
except his head feels like his hair is bruised.

He smirks because he'll be the talk for sure,
though it best not get back to dad. Outside,
she fakes a suffering look (You know, the blues),

but thinks she might be better seen as "fun"
so peps up, pumps in hand, and smiles wide.
They're young, have almost everything to lose,
and might not blame the other. Not the sun,

not booze.

Invisible Fish

The guide at the slide show asks us
who can see the fish.
Each, in our own Alaskas,
could guess, but only a wish

we could be surer rises.
Reluctant to raise a hand,
our total silence comprises
the fear of reprimand:

an ax-headed thought might swim:
a stone mistaken for a trout
below the ruffled scrim
of the run would leave no doubt

how Texan, how far we are
from nature. The hush confirms
our ignorance: we'd mar
the world with hooks and worms.

His silhouette's afloat
behind the projector's boulder,
light swirling hotel motes
before him: silt, lit golden.

If he's the fisherman,
then we're the fish aware
of shadows, movement on
the shore, hunger and fear

our needle north from birth
and sex to death. He waits
as patiently the earth
holds steady on its plates

till a laser pointer now
points fish fish fish, undresses
the innocence of how
we hid within our guesses.

The last few slides, and on
come the lights. The river
evaporates. We're gone
like fish out of water shiver.

II

For the Christian Angler

If God is angler, Christ the fly, and we
the trout that He by gentle cast befriend,
then how to justify this thorny gift?

Mere hunger seems to ravage liberty.
Over the sins of falling Time, His mend
across the current, boulders, and wind will lift

our eyes to a beautiful illusion, achieve
in us the faith we choose our heaven's end.
We rise to an immaculate dead drift.

Catch and release me. Make, if I believe,
short shrift.

River Prayer

Non è fantin che sì sùbito rua
col volto verso il latte, se si svegli
molto tardato da l'usanza sua
      —Paradiso 30:82–84

Our river, which art might make known your powers
other than prayer, the mouth where all the falling
ends in a whisper? The shell of the aural sea

might not at first receive the crafted hours,
the cries that turn back in a tidal crawling
toward a source as the child delivered, free,

rejects his freedom in the world, devours
love and loves. Graceful mother do not grieve
when your child at last moves toward eternity

from home. He will return in time. Believe
you me.

"Trout that swim"

Wait to wade. Streamside, kneel, retrieve a stone
from the wet edge. Beneath slither the nymphs
of flies, a moving prehistoric sketch.

They scuttle their inept attempts at bone
to undermine the light, your sight, and hints
of what will cast successfully. Yet you catch

that shine, that peacock herl. A small refusal
whets wish, is charming as a timid prin-
cess. Understand a rock if you would match

(undistracted by the bobbing ousel)
this hatch.

The Rio Hondo

Upper

By June the record snows released a cold
torrent of water bulging over each falls
like the molten glass contemporary art

the Taos galleries gush over. We're sold
on twisted color trapped in shaped globules:
a tropical bird or jellyfish, a heart.

What little blue the river holds must come
by open sky through green and canyon walls
contributing their igneous colorchart.

Up at the Ski Valley source I drink, both dumb
and smart.

Lower

This stretch, too fast, brown, casts a dry-fly curse
with summer runoff at a decade-high.
My favorite local fishing spot. No worry

that anyone will find it: who reads verse?
On the crumbling bank, think what to do, fret, sigh,
despair on wishing (a river's never sorry)

for nature´s sympathy. This muddy knowing
threads almost nothing through my empty eye.
From the car, I take my lunch two hours early,

a pen, a notebook. I watch the river going.
No hurry.

The Little Rio Grande

Past spruce, down meadows, and I'm trickling up
a storm of cottonwoods. I run beside
the road the redneck rides his 4×4 on,

then along Route 518 until I fall
into trout-filled acequias, the pride
of Rancho. Except that every other moron

tosses his beer cans here. I join big water
at the gorge and watch these lowlife rafters (and guide)
get back to nature. Who's the oxymoron?

All this leisure, hard to believe we've got a
war on.

The Rio Grande

At the John Dunn Bridge some locals almost let
their baby drown. He drifted off, face-down,
diaper-up, ten yards, before we cried

(we saw him first) our warning to upset
their fun. Mid-summer's river's a sluggish brown.
The waters start to clear and rapids subside.

Balloonists dip below the famous ridge
at dawn to touch the water, and rise to crown
the mesa. Just a mile from here, beside
himself, last week, another Gorge Bridge

suicide.

Pot Creek

I took a dozen Anasazi shards
and left a hundred more behind because
I'm not the only one who likes an antique,

a bit of history that no one guards
(the funding for the site expired). And laws?
Abandoned land, the posted stream, the meek

remains of art, once kingdom to a few
abstract expressionists: these gave me pause.
But then I walked back to the car to sneak

my rod. The brown trout leapt from, at my cue,
Pot Creek.

Cause

Daddy, she says, the Mallards are pretending
they're planes. We need the elegant dumb luck
a child makes of cause. And one might think

of the jet that made the Hudson River landing
last year. Like ducklings on a metal duck
the ring-necked passengers burst out on the brink.

Some kind of William Carlos Williams depending
upon a ditched wet vehicle's surprise
of emptiness and waiting, suspended in ink.

A bird descends, and even God is baptized.
Thirst, drink.

Nathaniel Hawthorne at Niagara Falls

Our Frenchman leaned out the coach window and roared!
I felt like running head-long into the mist but sat
till we rolled into town, eyes closed, feigning boredom.
The old black footman took my coat and hat.
I asked the dinner hour.

Such has often been my apathy,
when objects long desired come within my grasp.
My mind then grew benumbed, sad, drowsy.
I smoked a cigar, neither slow nor fast,
and lingered like an epicure.

After supper, I strolled toward Goat Island,
stopped at the toll house, and wandered in to stall
among the beaded trifles made of deer skin,
great mounted beasts, the news from Montreal—
two days old, or older.

Finally, at the blast of wind and spray
I could not quite appreciate the falls' renown:
the joys of hope had turned to memory
and a wretched disappointment weighed me down.
I turned from the roar.

Never was the summer night more calm with stars.
How could I sleep when I heard this endless breath
crossing the mouth of God. The cataract rush jars
the casements here, a mile away. And yet
I slept within the hour.

Sonnet on Time

You recognize what weight the river carries
imagining your body swims to learn
the current. Then, but what below would bury
your errors, even troubles? What lusts burn
and might be baptized, raised surprised to the height
of love, floating? Earth the rivers shoulder
is imperceptibly removed like night
believing in its wisdom, as grows older
each star awakening to know its wrecked
and fixed position in a myth. Higher,
we ask how time exists beyond effect:
marrow in bone, electrons on a wire.
The river rises to meet the falling rain.
Whose strokes make Time sway on its gold watch chain?

III

The Death of Adam

Oh, they had slaughtered animals and held
those limp and tedious portions in their arms,
the meat's red rising into strangest violet.
And all had cut themselves by accident
or fallen sick, some wishing they were dead.

This death wasn't sudden as with that first
son slain, abandoned to birds, and the second vanished.
He had lain there in his final days wanting
aloud for light or water. But now the rest
had come, and he was heavy as a limb
and stinking. Might they just burn him on a spit?
But too much time had passed. No need for a tomb
or rite, and death had not become an art.

The body before them marbling on its bed,
they knew only that they would never know.
Yet a habit of attention had begun.

She picked a lily and laid it on his chest
and then another after dirt and rock
they heaped upon him skull to nails to hide
this shame they could not clothe. Somehow they prayed.

Echo

I couldn't understand the thing he told me.
He said he couldn't make it any clearer:
I'd rather die of thirst than have you hold me.

Hold me, I said. His elegance consoled me,
and his refusal made him all the dearer.
I couldn't understand. The thing he told me,

twice (how could anyone repeat it?), bowled me
over. I put it to myself, and queerer:
I'd rather die of thirst than have you hold me?

Just look at me at least, I wished. Behold me!
You wish, he mocked and looked toward his mirror.
I couldn't understand the thing he told me.

Perhaps our likenesses, not love, controlled me.
Then something turned and spoke in me. I hear her:
I'd rather die of thirst then have you hold me

is what I should have said to draw him nearer.
We have in common our redundant error.
I couldn't understand the thing he told me:
I'd rather die of thirst than have you hold me.

Elegy for a Suicide

She always liked to blow the candles out. Fact:
there's only so much you can do with friction
and an intentional hand before the hand burns.
The sound that scissors make in a child's hand
while crunching construction paper aches when she grows
older. Even popcorn ceilings lose that style,
that feeling of a cereal freshly drowned in milk.
Ah, the white beneath things. And the black below that.
We come down from bunk beds. We come down from
the funky reds and yellows of the spring's Summer tanager
gone in fall. We fail to see the most vivid birds
high in the trees on the other side of leaves.

Where did those sad seeds come from or how take root?
Her departure spun out of some samara down into
                                            a maple
shadow that shadows well into night's sweet syrup.
This speechless country pretends we have no knife,
no guns in the bedroom, no large car for escaping
or crashing over hard hillsides or into houses.
We stuff our faces, blank as pills, with pills.
No one wants to open that book, but it's a book.

Ars Proverbium

Proverbs master the man.
He longs to be simple who writes a proverb.
A proverb well-chosen for a tombstone is a life.
He that does not understand a proverb is the hole in a
wire hanger.
The weakest proverb is great, though a great proverb
is never weak.
There is no weak proverb.
A proverb unspoken is a prayer.
A proverb unwritten is a curse.
A proverb in the mouth of a fool is a proverb.
A fool in the mouth of a proverb is not necessarily a fool.
A parent speaking a proverb to a child is a barking dog.
Psalms are lamps, proverbs mirrors.
A fool seeks out the exceptions of a proverb.
Many proverbs spoken in a short time mark trouble.

Memento Mori

—Know thyself.

Identity is only ultimate.
Don't wait until the blowflies interpose.
You live when you have reckoned yourself dead.

The wine-dark sea is peaceful violet
and doesn't seem a storm or carry foes.
Identity is only ultimate

come undertows or tsunamis to bed.
Only when your heart starts to decompose
you live. When you have reckoned yourself dead,

you might rely on God to pay your debt.
At epic's end we know Telemachos'
identity is only, ultimate-

ly, the son within the father's epithet.
A man of many turns must know (God knows)
you live when you have reckoned yourself dead,

when flesh at best can only altar it:
this moving story coming to a close.
Identity is only ultimate.
You live when you have reckoned yourself dead.

Perspective on Might

Superior to the philosopher of God's absence,
the avalanche is patient above those pines
it might sublimely clean its teeth with.
At the lip of the highest peak snow accumulates
on a dead man's moustache like a dead man's moustache.
Repetition isn't funny to the dead man who never
made it to that bar in Champagne for champagne
or to the avalanche whose time has almost come.
We might consider how scale means to climb
or to remove the scales from a dead creature
with this precious, precise violence we call a knife.
A philosopher needs a sharp knife to cut the cord
of pride hanging her like a Christmas ornament
from her parachute caught in the trees of the supernatural.
After all, God is present as that last snowflake settling
on the lip, the tickle which has come a long way
to now. From afar it looks so soft. Even the knife.

Roadside Memorial

Was this the speed they crossed the double line,
this cross the white response to an X of black
that struck the window smashed below the pine?
The needles might have dropped their mortal fact

to hush the moaning scene. Or all the car
was awed before the jolted, echoing wood.
The injured grass, toward the highest star,
began to right itself as best it could.

Fall

The high plains long last light last night painted
our patio the heightened pink of passion,
sky brushed to a slutty blush, acquainted
with shadows. All summer it had been our fashion
to wait until the stars and Mars came rolling
over before we'd take our cocktail gazes
inside. But an omen was coming on, controlling
our plot. The lurid figure still amazes:

a wrecker on a wrecker passed, created
a ruckus with the racks, chains, antidoting
the juniper sedative rest of our rest. Defeated,
we fled the yellow lights, hoping nothing
coming from the warning. Summer's pleasure
over, we buried ourselves in bed like treasure.

Et Cetera

From town you walked home lit and, laughing, pulled
me out of bed for stars that looked like salt
or holes of light in black or jewels to you.
You took my hand and drug me to the roof
to understand the heavens come so close.
The bar-flung drivers turned their radios
against the calm of Iowa, and faded.
The crickets drank the dew and serenaded.
The stars back toward the lukewarm college town
were lost to haze. We kissed, I led you down
the stairs, forgot the stars, and didn't care
what had you pointing there. You said, *I swear
to you, et cetera*. Your mouth was sweet
and made me sick in love with our defeat.

At the Hospice

You made a funny joke about a nun,
and we both laughed. But then you started crying.
You laughed at death but couldn't take the dying.
Your wife was dead. Only thirty minutes gone.
Sad, serious and habited, the nun
had passed the doorway, and the joke came flying.
We couldn't help but laugh, I said. We're trying . . .
You couldn't answer, doubled over sighing.
Beside the bed, her wristwatch lay undone.
To your shoes you said, Is this how life goes on?
The watch was running strong where it was lying.
Your wife just lay there, thirty minutes gone,
awaiting the mortician and his son
who finally came. And there was no denying.

Good God

They ate of the tree of knowledge, then they fell
toward labor, labor, and the existential.
I don't divine God's cause or will, as well.
And worse, I blame the providential.
At best I hear an ocean in a shell.
By candle light I wax self-referential.
I mind my manners, modesty, and swell,
ridiculous as fig leaves, confidential.

Why do I do the same old raising hell
when repetition loves the consequential?
Be good. Don't touch that tree. I see how they fell
for the lie, the yes we can, the presidential.
Here comes the cancer and the prison cell.
Life is knowing dying as essential.

IV

Pope Innocent X (Velázquez)

You can almost see in his face the organ meats
but minus the gleam one gets on the internet.
The Doria Pomphilj haze come through

the grimy skylight in this small room meets
that gaze above his trough of a pink cape, yet
darker, near blood. One thinks he must eschew

Velázquez, children, or even the surprise
Bacon will make of him. He pays his debt
to portraiture—this sacerdotal *et tu*,

the surly beard, and art's divining eyes
too true.

At Dante's Tomb

One suffers disappointment at such times
and places, baffled by the heat of Ravenna.
After a week in Rome writing our rhymes,
we were puzzled by that arrow-shaped antenna

obstructing the terrace view in Fiesole
and pointing to Brunelleschi's dome below
in Florence where one angel grieves each day
and the other looks to where we've come to know

little: little facts of the archaic
Theodoric our poet might have despised,
and little tiles of the stateliest mosaic.
He never rested where he now abides.

The maker lies here somewhere in this marble.
It is a wonder that we do not marvel.

Liquid Italy

The summer the Bolognesi went crazy
for the spritz with Aperol,
I stuck to chilled and sweating prosecco
though switched to sangiovese
and later couldn't refuse a little red fizzy
(one tries to stay hydrated)
in a second floor flat in Casalecchio
where we three poets had been invited
for a full-blown home-cooked supper
by Mina, Italian grandmother,
who had been warming up the apartment
all day, and what I got to compliment
that perfect 100 degree heat we wallowed in,
Fahrenheit our God, water the religion,
and our Italian host seeming nearly heroic
when she brought it iceless, stoic,
to us seated at the table next to the little kitchen
with the big stove where water boiled, rabid
for the fettuccini while a ragu of wild rabbit
simmered, and only one window of three
was open but no breeze graced us anyway
so our shirts hung like wet laundry
the Italians hang from a balcony
or windows (Oh, if someone could have only
hung me out a window), what I got
was a wild boar tortellini
drowned in a salty chicken broth
for starters and then the steaming fettuccine
and saltless bread to soak up the last of the sauce,

and when the gelato finally came
even that added fat to the heat and warmed
our tongues with vanilla liqueur and cream
so thick no ice crystal could hope to form,
of course with grappa and nocino following it all,
and/or limoncello (who could recall?)
thinking the burn up our nasal passages
and down our throats might distract us
while the golden hillside wheatfields drying
bleached under the last of the purifying
Emilia-Romagna sun declining
by, we prayed, degrees
that evening, and the figs in the trees
and the grapes green and waxing clearer
were just beginning to fatten at the height
of summer on the longest day of the year.

Ignored Woodwork in Old Churches

Outside the intertwining diamond rings
on a saint's dress in a painting, beyond the frame
next to the chapel where the guidebook
mistook Dante's hell for purgatory,
his suicidal Harpies for Man-Doves,
just past the Brunelleschi crucifix,
the seats where the preaching friars sit
are carved with scrolls and heads of animals
or men or monsters in between.
I want to know what kind of wood
and how the hinges will convert the seat
into a stall where a monk can stand for a while
to worship, tucked neatly into his niche
like the saint he is or may become.
Look closely on the armrest and you see
the pinprick wormholes perpetrated
over centuries. Softer than fetus flesh,
each worm extended the finger of its hunger,
and like a nearly imperceptible symbol of
a crucifixion nail, drove its being
into boring. Almost no one notices
to the left of the nave where the naïve are drawn
like moths. Small sacrifice to drop their euros
toward the bookstore for remembrance—or
toward a little light above an altar
where we do not bow but stand and like
the way the stained glass seems to make
each of us a cracking chrysalis restored
to what we always must have been becoming.

The Race of the Candles

I climb that I may be no longer blind.
    —Purgatorio 26:58

By noon, we've hiked one half the mountain road
toward Saint Ubaldo, up from Gubbio,
this ancient town, her citizens in blue
or black or yellow shirts, red kerchiefs for
their throats a harmony among the crowd,
the masses who sing, drunkenly cling. Bells ring
from stone towers, drawing to the piazza
bands of flutes, horns, and drums. The people war
among themselves like children playing war,
their colors representative: the saints
of masons, merchants, or necessary farmers:
Antonio, Giorgio, then beloved Ubaldo,
the patron of this festival, this town
we've left below, departing for an hour
or two, uncertain what we're looking for
up here, how long our walk, or how they'll run
this evening's race, their strongest men bearing
the sacred wooden candles ten feet tall
upon their shoulders (a dozen to each *cero*),
racing toward the Saint who loves them all.

Toward his pickled, dried, and shrunk remains—
Ubaldo encased in glass atop the altar.
According to those austere chapel frescoes,
he held reluctantly the bishop's reins
and, horseback, led outnumbered Umbrians

to necessary war, but more, forgiveness.
We can almost see the square, past cypresses,
through the hillside bushes clutching ditches
below this winding road, and you, my new wife,
trying to see, say you love your new life.

As if the worshipping world approves your bliss,
a distant roar arises like a wave,
another, then one more, and now we know
the candles have been hauled from where they're kept
in the church, carried down the granite steps
into the stone piazza. The noon sun burns,
the young men lift the candles, like caskets turned
on end and into sudden wooden towers,
balanced, offered up for heaven's sanction,
the pealing bells, the shouts for half an hour.
They've come to bless their patron saint again
by the light of the highest candle of the sun.
We didn't understand the schedule, know
that noon begins the revelry below.

Gubbio, the town subject to fogs,
ancient home of Francis' famous wolf
who made his peace with man and lesser dogs,
precipitous home to flashy festivals
of crossbows aiming for the truest mark
(the center bloody as a human heart),
of truffles white and aching with the flavor
of pure decay below an oaken fountain,
of candles carried with the love of labor,
of saintly love more zealous on the mountain

than hidden in a bushel, these candles run
Ingino's thousand feet. Gubbio,
home of the greatest poet's proudest friend:
Dante's Oderisi who, with pen
in hand, his muscles aching, the whole day,
bent over a page, over an immense *I*
illuminating ink into an image,
a snake and ivy-strangled pillar holding
its own, a decorated character
for launching testaments, God's character,
a border rising to a story, an homage
a gold-leaf halo renders holy, an *I*
rising beyond the skin of pages onto
a mountain ledge of words and drawn into
another skin: literal ecstasy.

Here we have risen by wedding, honeymoon,
and travel to our mountain afternoon.
The curves and trees of the steep hillside occlude
our view. We kneel and rise and kneel once more,
to no avail. We hear the piazza roar
and see its churning, bright periphery
shift like a moving wave that, spilled to shore,
pulls back to darkness, heaving mystery.
Like this, time's shadow moves until the laps
repeat themselves upon a moment's place
through miracle of memory. Perhaps
the shoulder's edge, the hunger in your eyes
restores to me another story: noon
when Dante and his friend Farese walked,
condemning the excessive love of food

and drink, corrupting earthly goods, and talked
of memory, but more the coming sweet
new style, the intellect of ladies, gentle,
thin elegance of wintering cranes in flight
forming into Vs and simply rendered.

And then, a candle races down a street!
Can we turn back, go down for what we're missing?
I'm torn, halfway between the host below—
this invisible rabble, these revel-loving living—
and the hill, the grave above, still Saint Ubaldo,
who built on the ruins of Iguvium
God's fortress, a city lifted toward religion,
among fresh flowers, mostly roses, laid
in his simple chapel telling all his story:
the legend of a life and death remembered
in frescoes, pamphlets, voices in the nave
praying, preparing for the coming glory
of candles to the citizens surrendered,
not coming yet, but topped with puppet saints
just down the mountainside and carried through
the streets, each racing with its retinue.

Should we turn back? What do we want? Descent?
We want to howl among the half-drunk men,
white throats, red scarves, these human candles all
ardent to carry the burden of a saint
of eight proud centuries, now passing by
the offerings of warm biscotti, wine,
and water, a holy meal half for the show,
half nourishment, and passing by each wall,

stacked, mortared, white and gray flecked, sparkling stones
hewn from this very mountain on which we stand
to serve as streets and walls, so set by hands
building a story, passed to generations
passing another candle hurtling through
the crowded street, candles almost crashing,
passing, passing, passing the faces passing
away, running, shadowed shoulder to shoe,
telling the hour, the inextricable tie
to work, the colors, blood. In short, we die.

And yet, to be exactly here, to hear
somewhere in the bush behind a sparrow stir
the present into place. And, feathery,
I fall into another reverie.

What was it that you said in our hotel
the other night? Perugia, warm, we held
each other drunk and glistening after love.
You called me by a nearby city's name,
touching my ear. You meant to make me laugh,
but I felt built of great stones, bread, and fountains—
all Abraham-and-Isaac on the mountain,
God-exhausted, purified and saved,
the knife of evening lowering beside us.

But never have we been more love-alive
than on this simple precipice which guides us
halfway to the death of who we are
today, toward Saint Ubaldo's rest, displayed
to teach us this dry mountain road must rise

to lift us all upon his bone-cold altar,
white marble artfully carved, fearfully made,
our mortal burden more beautiful because
we love and worship beyond knowledge and time.

So worldly, are we doomed to chase a boulder
down the hill of school, our lessons learned,
of work—or can we learn to love our lots,
wear scarlet on our throats to signify
our end, wear each red sound around our words,
carry our less than subtle candle high?

The bells below now hold their tongues, the piazza
empties, the unruly run through the streets begun.
Turning away, I take you by the hand,
and pull you closer still, the candle of
our affection humbled under noon. We stand
here in the new life we have found, and love
each face upon the other's neck. Content,
we both let go and turn toward the road,
toward our Saint. Again begins the climb
out of our shadows, taking our time.

A Crown for Meghan

As if God's future thundered on my past.
    —Elizabeth Barrett Browning

I.

Our eleventh year—you change and haven't changed.
We multiply. You gave me a daughter, twice,
and we mature, familiar and strange.
Remember that premarital advice

your aunt and uncle gave us when we asked?
Have fun, a sense of humor. Be flexible.
Watching you make the bed, I crane to catch
your moves and make myself the spectacle.

Do I pin you down, or up, or misconstrue
when I lift from Hawthorne, Ovid, Homer? I poach
the heart that fed the courtiers: Miss Blue,
My Windblown Dove, my Flame in Flames. You
                                    approach,

seem tame, but vanish among two streams. The stealth.
Amanuensis, I call you Mine Own Self.

II.

Amanuensis, I call you Mine Own Self
and see my odd reflection in the gems
I polish. Pity me, who cannot help
a crown besmeared with prints despite attempts

to keep my hand away. I fly to craft
when I should kiss your subtle feet. Pardon
the art, the work I think I do, and laugh
at me, the old class clown from kindergarten.

By now you know by heart, O quick apprentice,
my act, my audience. At the kitchen sink
you stand there washing vegetables, a tempest
in your hands and in your hair the stars. Your ink-

blue, lawless eyes draw me. Sweet drink, command
this desert wanderer who wants your hand.

III. —*Draw me. We will run after Thee.*

The desert wanderers who wanted your hand,
those brawling, coarse slang-mongers…poets past
and present missing you, bring gifts like a band
of suitors wealthiest with want. At last,

my brother-measurers who toil to make
you swoon would better offer up white rice.
Because they long to honor you, let them take
as recompense our rose-strewn cake, a slice.

Those smilers cannot look into the sun
without a screen. I'd rather be blinded
and let you lead me by the hand, undone
like an exiled man who loses life to find it,

while the minor, major, and the jealous wonder.
Other people are the world's width asunder.

IV.

Other people are the world's width asunder.
We practice love the God of nature taught us,
and put the other first, above, both under-
standing at last that I'm your Deodatus,

studied in the Song of Songs and Texas,
the right hand here, the left beneath your head,
my thirsty kisses circling like a necklace
to your doves of eyes, your fawns on lilies fed.

Nobody ever had a wife but me.
And nobody a husband save my Dove.
Fall on my eyes, wildflower of purity,
Cosmos. Now help me understand how Love

has her own omniscient form which I pretend.
To gain the wind's perspective, I ascend.

V. Away

To gain the wind's perspective, I ascend
to the topmast of a salt ship, would rather leap
and break my neck than write as if an end
of you existed. It seems as if a sheet

of paper might be the veil dividing us,
a sail, my ordinary life head-long,
so perfectly untrammeled as it is.
Why rhyme, or measure black, white, weak and strong?

The treeless, fierce-sunshining, irksome lanes
of the plains like oceans break my aspirations. Where
are those tender anxieties, when you leaned
on my arm and needed its superfluous care?

I'd come down from this rigging's highest rung
if I could know your name in every tongue.

VI.

If I could know your name in every tongue,
I might be satisfied, hushed, stillness ours.
Have not the moments of our marriage sung
in calm, substantial, and most silent hours?

In Heaven there will be no metric nonsense,
labored and artificial, no pronouns minced.
We are already one another's conscience.
Your verb's auxiliary, I am convinced

it's happiness to need you, equally
pervading presence and an absence. Possessed
by your name's rise and fall, the quality
which is and is not you, I'll weave a nest:

a natural crown for you to dwell on, proud
mockingbird, my poetry aloud.

VII.

Mockingbird, my poetry aloud
in your voice sounds me, like me, and the chaste
Penelope, the queen of a theft allowed
and more dear mirror, most at home. Chased

and caught by no one else, thou, unforgettablest
pedestaled, understood, the very sight
of wilderness, change me, beloved blessed
with vehement and faithful love. Kiss, cite

these precious next two words: I'm home.
I traveled to return. Here, lie down, rest.
I'll make the bed next time. Our home
is shipshape, hungry for a mess. The rest?

You're my couplet met, familiar love still strange
in our eleventh year. You change but have not changed.